CONTENTS

W9-AQG-854

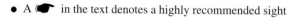 • A ☞ in the text denotes a highly recommended sight

London

LONDON & THE LONDONERS

For centuries, London has been a favorite destination of travelers from around the globe. They've come for many reasons, from invasion to vacation, and they've certainly never been let down. The theater, from the medieval Globe to the present day National Theatre, has been a delight for generations of visitors, as have the miles of corridors in magnificent museums, the art exhibitions, stately homes, churches, and parklands. At the dawn of the new millennium, even more pleasures can be added to London's traditional charms.

There's the revitalized street life with all the sidewalk cafés, buskers, and markets. The Ferris wheel on the Thames provides staggering views that span the centuries from the Tower of London to the Millennium Dome. The controversial new British Library has turned out to be a great improvement, but you can still visit the Old Reading Room in the British Museum to pay your respects to the Library's illustrious past. And the nightlife and shopping have been improving steadily since London has grudgingly accepted that some people like to party all night long and shop on Sunday.

London's the kind of town visitors can picture themselves living in, and everyone can imagine visiting again and again. Londoners are, if not warm and demonstrative, among the most polite in the world. You will be called "sir" and "madam" regularly. Pleases and thank-yous will ring out from behind shop counters and from small London children. No one will cut in line in front of you. And you will learn to recognize the exquisite moment of hesitation during which you are expected to say, "No, please, *you* first." Drivers and taxis are a different story, and although they both seem determined to run you down in the road, for the most part a taxi will respond to a raised arm and take you wherever you want to go, in great style and comfort.

And there are so many places to go. If it's history you fancy, try the Tower of London, Kensington Palace, Westminster Abby, or the Museum of London. There's no better city for theater: Go to the half-price ticket booth in Leicester Square and pick a play for the evening, you'll be amazed at the variety of choice. Check out the newly refurbished Royal Opera House, or visit the gorgeous Royal Albert Hall for classical music or the Cirque de Soleil. There are museums for every possible taste and interest, even quirky ones for fans of old medical instruments; and the teenage taste for the macabre is well-catered to in Madame Tussauds Chamber of Horrors and the London Dungeon. If it's the great outdoors you crave, go watch the red deer in Richmond Park, boat on the Serpentine in Hyde Park, or feed the pelicans in St. James's; there's no city that can boast more verdant greenlands than London. The playwright Ben Jonson's words from the 16th century have not lost currency: "Our scene is London, 'cause we would make it known, no country's mirth is better than our own."

The parks can be enjoyed all year round: London has a benign climate with mild winters during which much of the greenery continues to thrive. Lately, the summers have suffered from spells of torrid temperatures, but you can always find a cool breeze and refreshing shade somewhere. Just beware of the underground on the hot days and avoid the *un*-air conditioned restaurants and hotels — there are still plenty of them here. While the actual amount of rainfall in London doesn't live up to its reputation, there are plenty of romantically gloomy and wet days to keep the populace tut-tutting over the weather, a favorite topic of conversation.

London, London burning bright... London's twilight skyline is a brilliant reflection of the city's many splendors.

You won't mind putting up with whatever the skies may bring when you're walking around London, and do be sure to walk. You may cheat yourself even by taking the delightful double-decker buses that provide such a wonderful perspective on London. For it is by wandering on foot that you will happen upon some surprising treasures: a whipping post and stocks in Shoreditch, street lamp standards with cherubs talking on an old-fashioned telephone on the Victoria Embankment, a statue of Sir Thomas More with golden face. The blue plaques on the buildings are fascinating, revealing that legendary figures such as Oscar Wilde, Mozart, Karl Marx, Florence Nightingale, Vincent Van Gogh, or Ellen Terry once lived there.

You may as well take your time when you're in London, because there's no chance that you'll see it all. There are layers upon layers of London, rising up to today from Roman

Londinium to Victoria's reign to post-Blitz: The past is always present in this city. As you round a corner in the City, you'll suddenly find yourself staring up at Christopher Wren's Monument to the Fire of London, now strangely dwarfed by the skyscrapers all around. An angel designed by Nicholas Hawksmoor floats above the entrance to the Bank tube station. After checking out the gladrags at Vivien Westwood's on the King's Road, you may come upon the wooden doors that hide the 18th-century Moravian burial ground where the graves are divided by sex and marital status. Keep your eyes wide when you walk around London and don't forget to look up occasionally, or you'll miss some of the most beautiful statues, friezes, and just plain eccentricities that generations of Londoners have devised and appreciated.

The stoic glare of a Queen's Guard in winter uniform in front of Buckingham Palace.

London is enjoying a great boom of popularity these days, and indeed, is often styled "The Capital of Europe." With the amazing ethnic diversity here — the end result of centuries of empire-building and ocean-crossing — it could just as easily be called "The Capital of the World." African, American, Arab, Australian, Caribbean, Chinese, Filipino, Indian, Thai — there are neighborhoods for all nationalities, and all

Historic Landmarks

Albert Memorial: Neo-Gothic Victorian extravagance, recently restored to its former glory.

Buckingham Palace: An old estate from 1702 was rebuilt by John Nash; further refinements added and subtracted throughout the next century.

County Hall: Started in 1911, it wasn't officially opened until 1922; see it from the north bank of the river; now contains the London Aquarium.

Hampton Court Palace: Building started in 1515 and continued into the 18th century. Combination of period designs and features.

Kenwood and Chiswick House: Classic Palladian designs by the famous Adams brothers of the 18th century.

Lloyd's of London: Sir Richard Roger's designed high-tech, high drama modern high-rise serves as a symbol of the 1980s.

Millennium Dome: The much-debated, often vilified structure seeks to mark 1000 years of British progress.

Natural History Museum: Splendid architectural achievements both inside and out, completed in 1880.

Roman Wall at the Barbican: One of the few remnants of Rome's Londinium, circa A.D. 50–60.

Southwark Cathedral: Remains of 13th- and 14th-century Gothic architecture can be seen here, plus stained glass windows depicting Shakespeare's characters.

St. Barthomew the Great: A collection of bits from the 12th, 15th, and 17th centuries, with Victorian restorations at this church.

St. Paul's Cathedral: Christopher Wren's masterpiece and memorial, started after the Great Fire of 1666.

Tower of London: London's oldest fortress, built by William the Conqueror in the 1070s by the remains of a Roman wall; Tudor and Victorian additions.

Westminster Abby: Begun in 1060 by Edward the Confessor, restored and added to over the centuries.

nationalities in every neighborhood. And most happily, they remembered to bring the recipes from the old country.

Of the estimated ten million visitors each year, there are plenty who have no interest in either culture or history, and they too are amply amused by London. The nightlife is brilliant, the restaurants plentiful, and a whole generation of hip new designers and style mongers are being monitored by fashionistas the world over. London has never dressed so well, eaten so well, or partied so hard...except perhaps during the swinging sixties, or the roaring twenties, or the naughty Edwardian age, or the elegant Elizabethan times, or...well, you get the picture. It's *still* the place to be.

Despite the horrendous expense of just eating and sleeping

in this city, despite the traffic and the pollution, and the great distances between boroughs, London keeps calling people back. Whatever the reasons they have for loving London (and no matter how hateful it can be sometimes) love it they do and have done for generations. William Shakespeare could have been referring to his adopted hometown of London when he wrote, "Age cannot wither her, nor custom stale her infinite variety."

London's pristine elegance — detailed down to its stately phone booths.

A BRIEF HISTORY

Although Julius Caesar, in his ever-expanding quest for Empire, landed in England twice — in 56 and 55 B.C. — he came, he saw, and he left without leaving any trace of a settlement. It remained for the Emperor Claudius and his Roman legions in A.D. 43 to conquer the island and build what was likely the first bridge — at about the same place as the present London Bridge — over the Thames, establishing the trade port of Londinium.

Roman engineers built a basilica, a forum, temples, and many grand villas for the population of around 50,000 in the area that is now known as the City. A temple of Diana once stood on the same hill that St Paul's Cathedral and its earlier incarnations have occupied since 604. The Romans also built roadways, forts, villas, and an enormous amphitheater that was excavated near Guildhall in 1988.

Roman rule was often challenged, most violently in the bloody uprising led by the Iceni tribe's Queen Boudicca, whose statue can be seen at the northern end of Westminster Bridge. Partly in response to this violent insurrection, it was soon deemed prudent by the Romans to start building massive stone walls around the city. Parts of these walls were excavated around the Barbican area, the best chunk being outside the Museum of London; inside one can see fascinating recreations of Roman daily life.

From Angles to Normans

As the Roman Empire began its decline and fall, the legions were recalled from London in 410 and thus began the Dark Ages. Londonium became a ghost town, slowly buried under silt and grass, as other invaders avoided the walled area. Eventually, over the North Sea came the Saxons to build

Lundenwic, and after a brief return to paganism, the seeds of Christianity sown by the late Romans began to take sprout in London again. St.Ethelbert, the first Christian king, dedicated a small church built of timber to St. Paul, and during the succeeding centuries it was destroyed and rebuilt no less than four times as London grew again into a thriving port.

The Saxon kings were constantly at battle with Viking and Danish invaders, and when the Danes won the day and put King Canute on the throne in 1016, London unseated Winchester as the capital of the kingdom. In the 1040s, Westminster Abbey was built by Edward the Confessor, a pious though ineffectual king. When the Norman army of William the Conqueror was victorious at the Battle of Hastings in 1066, King William began the centuries-long tradition of being crowned at the Abbey. William respected London's great wealth and commercial energy, and shrewdly forged a relationship with the Church and citizenry that would benefit all concerned, especially the monarchs. The king began the monumental work that would become the Tower of London — at first a mere earth and wood castle — which he eventually enlarged into a magnificent palace-fortress, with the statuesque White Tower a symbol of the Conqueror's power.

Feudal England

During the early Middle Ages London's influence grew rapidly while the kings of England were diverted by wars in France and Crusades to the Holy Land. Under King Henry I, its citizens won the right to choose their own magistrates, and during the reign of the absentee king, Richard the Lionheart, the elective office of Lord Mayor of London was created. In 1215, Richard's brother, John, was forced to bow to the defiant noblemen assembled in the meadow of Runnymede (outside Windsor) and set his seal to the Magna Carta. This historic breakthrough in the struggle against tyranny had the incidental effect of confirming the City of London's municipal autonomy.

England's medieval monarchs could not expect blind loyalty from the citizens of London. Their strong trade and craft guilds, which still exist today, created a self-determinism and power that often resulted in rebellions. The Palace of Westminster became the seat of government, and one of the reputed reasons for its chosen site was that its riverside location meant that a mob could never surround the building.

Despite a grim history, the Tower of London is London's greatest historical sight.

By 1340 London's population was around 50,000, but in 1348 disaster struck. The Black Death swept across Eurasia, killing some 75 million people. Details of the horrors in London are scarce, and although there are no accurate figures on the final death toll, it is thought that almost half of London succumbed to the disease.

More than 150 years later London still scarcely overflowed the square-mile Roman city limits. The momentous decision by King Henry VIII to break relations with Rome, however, not only gave birth to the Church of England, it also added new property in the form of seized monastery lands. Covent Garden, formerly a convent garden, is just one example of the choice church land that was freed for development.

The Elizabethan Era

Between the death of Henry VIII in 1547 and the coronation of his daughter Queen Elizabeth I in 1558, religious persecutions and political intrigues drained the kingdom of its coffers and influence. Under the 45-year reign of Elizabeth, England climbed to such heights of wealth and world power as had never been reached before, and London was the epicenter of this mighty kingdom. The defeat of the Spanish Armada in 1588 signaled the dawn of empire, as the victorious British Navy took to the seas in search of riches and began to cover the globe in colonial possessions. You can see a replica of Sir Francis Drake's flagship, the *Golden Hinde* in Southwark to get a sense of how difficult Elizabethan sea travel was.

The prosperity and relative peace of Elizabeth's reign was marked by the blossoming of English literature, with the incomparable Shakespeare as the jewel in the crown of literati who included as Christopher Marlowe, Francis Bacon, Edmund Spenser, and Ben Jonson. In 1599, the Globe Theater was established in Southwark, the scene of many crude entertainments such as bear-baiting and brothels. The original burned down within decades, but you can now enjoy watch-

The Seven Dials Sundial keeps time amidst the bustle of Covent Garden and Soho.

ing a play in an fantastically faithful recreation of the Globe in which Shakespeare worked with such fertility.

Revolution and Restoration

In contrast to Elizabeth I's glittering reign, her Stuart successors are remembered principally for their failures. In 1605 James I narrowly escaped assassination in the abortive Gunpowder Plot: Guy Fawkes was discovered in the cellars of the Houses of Parliament about to light the fuse that would have blown up the king at the opening of Parliament on 5 November. On the same date each year, effigies of Guy Fawkes are burned at bonfire parties and fireworks celebrations.

James I's son, Charles I, was even less popular than his father, and by attempting to dissolve Parliament, he plunged the country into Civil War. In 1642 the Royalists (the "Cavaliers"), supported by the aristocracy, went into battle against the Parliamentary forces. The "Roundheads," named after their short, round hairstyle, were supported by the tradesmen and the Puritans and led by Oliver Cromwell. The Royalists were finally defeated at Naseby in 1645. Some three and a half years later Charles I was found guilty of treason and beheaded in front of the Banqueting House, the only surviving remnant of the former Whitehall Palace.

Cromwell assumed power and abolished the monarchy, and for a short period Britain became a republic. In 1653 he declared himself Lord Protector and remained so until his death five years later. By 1660, the country had become disenchanted with the dreary dictatorship of Puritan rule. The monarchy was restored under Charles II, a great patron of the arts and sciences, whose exile in France had been spent studying and womanizing. Among his many mistresses was the actress Nell Gwynne, who was granted No. 79 Pall Mall as a royal gift, and is commemorated with a Blue Plaque on that site.

Disasters and Recovery

The relaxation of the punitive Puritan mores was not to be long enjoyed. In 1665, a terrible plague stalked London, killing an estimated 110,000 Londoners. Death, disease, and decay turned the once vibrant city into a hellish madhouse, in which piles of bodies were left on the streets until the carts that trundled along with the drivers crying "Bring out your dead" could pick them up to be buried. In fear of contagion, the sick were boarded up in their homes and left to perish of starvation and the plague.

No sooner had the city begun to recover from the disease than its festering medieval alleyways, which had encouraged the spread of disease, were swept away in the Great Fire of 1666. About 80 percent of the old City area was destroyed, with some 100,000 people made homeless. Incredibly, due to a speedy evacuation there were only eight recorded deaths. Sir Christopher Wren was appointed joint head of a commission to oversee the rebuilding of the new city, and though his grand schemes were never fully realized, he made a massive contribution to the new London, including rebuilding St. Paul's Cathedral and 51 other churches. The Monument, Wren's memorial to the Great Fire, provides stunning views to those with the strength to climb its 311 steps.

The final great confrontation between king and parliament involved King James II, brother of Charles I. A fervent Catholic, James attacked the Church of England and disregarded the laws of the land. However, the people of England had no stomach for cutting off another royal head, and in 1688 James was allowed to flee the country. The so-called Glorious (because peaceful) Revolution ushered in William of Orange and Mary II to the throne, and established a stable constitutional monarchy at last. William and Mary, seeking fresh air, established a royal retreat at Kensington Palace.

Georgian Greatness

During the 18th and early 19th centuries, London became the dynamic and erudite capital of a great world power. In the coffeehouses of the City and the West End such brilliant men of letters as Swift, Pope, and Samuel Johnson held forth. Handel, the prolific court composer of King George I, was at work on his operas, oratorios, and concertos. Kew Gardens and the British Museum were opened to the public; and classical Palladian architecture flourished.

But there was a dark side to London. Slums grew up south of the river and in the East End. The urban poor took to drink, adulterated gin being the cheapest tipple, and the crime rate soared. The works of William Hogarth, particularly *Gin Lane*, savagely depict the time when you could get "drunk for one penny, dead drunk for two pennies."

Overseas the Empire was burgeoning, until a tax dispute caused a rift between Britain and the American colonies. This escalated into a full-scale revolutionary war, and to the astonishment of King George III, the colonists won their fight for independence. Even worse, by the end of the 18th century, Britain was threatened

A statue of Oliver Cromwell stands guard in front of the Houses of Parliament.

with Napoleonic invasion. Admiral Lord Nelson ensured that Britannia would continue to rule the waves by disposing of the French fleet during the Battle of Trafalgar in 1805. Ten years later Britain's great military hero, the Duke of Wellington, put an end to Napoleon's ambitions once and for all at the Battle of Waterloo. By 1801 London had become the world's most populous city, with over a million people.

Victorian Empire

The crowning of the 18-year-old Queen Victoria in 1837 gave the name to the most prodigiously expansive age of this small island. The Empire-building that was started in Queen Elizabeth's day was taken to new heights in the 19th century. Ships filled with the bounty of the colonies brought in more than goods for trading to the docks of the East End; they also

The resolute figure of Winston Churchill — an immortalized symbol of London's amazing fortitude.

brought in the new languages, new cultures, and new citizens who have helped to shape this cosmopolitan city.

But the unchecked growth of the Empire and the explosive Industrial Revolution left a wide swath of victims behind. While the rich grew fatter on the spoils of the Empire, the lives of poor were desperately wretched, and the pen of Charles Dickens pricked many a middle-class conscience with his portrayal of the misery and hopelessness of the souls condemned to poverty in this prosperous city. London was now growing even more rapidly, and by 1861 it numbered some three million inhabitants. To house the newcomers continually pouring into the city looking for work, the East End slums expanded.

The boundaries of London were pushed well out into the countryside with the development of public transportation. Newly invented omnibuses, trains, and, in 1863, the world's first underground railway, created a new breed of London citizen — the commuter.

The Twentieth Century

The First World War left London's young generation sadly depleted, as the debacle dragged on and on. The sounds of shelling in France could be heard from England's coasts, and in 1915, the lumbering German Zeppelins dropped the first bombs on the city. This was a mere foretaste of what was to come 25 years later. Meanwhile, the inexorable expansion of the metropolis reached its peak in 1939, with 8.6 million people living in the Greater London area.

Hitler's Blitzkrieg rained bombs down on London between September 1940 and May 1941, during which London experienced a ghastly 57 consecutive nights of bombing. Between 1941 and 1944, the skies above the Thames were quiet. But in June 1944, the infamous rockets known as "doodlebugs" were launched and battered London until the last one fell in March 1945. By the end of the war the death toll was more than 30,000, with 3.5 million homes damaged or destroyed. Through it all strode Winston Churchill, the indomitable spirit of wartime London, and a living symbol of the amazing fortitude of the people of London. You can experience England's finest hour at the Cabinet War Rooms, the underground headquarters of the British war effort. Post-war Britain was spent clearing rubble and living frugally, while ugly modern skyscrapers went up in the barren bomb sites of the East End.

London enjoyed a huge boom of popularity in the 1960s, courtesy of the "youthquake" started by such classic 1960s figures as the Beatles and Twiggy, and continued by a steady stream of world-class rock and rollers, as well as the artists, photographers, movie-makers, and writers who chronicled the times. The explosion of the anarchic punk culture in the 1970s was followed by the rampant materialism of Thatcherism and Conservative party rule.

As the 20th century and the first millennium have drawn to a close, London has been feted in the international press as "Cool Britannia," the true capital of Europe, and one of the greatest cities on earth. The changes have been considerable: The New Labour party was elected in 1997, the same year the world stopped and mourned the death of Diana, Princess of Wales. The ancient, hereditary House of Lords was updated and dismantled, the Queen pays voluntary taxes, and property values continue to soar beyond reason. The Millennium Dome, that hotly debated "overturned tea cup" in the East End, is styled as the symbol of the new London, the London whose rich history is prologue to a prosperous present and a bright future. London is a place for all seasons, one which shall always be, as a 14th-century poet wrote, "the flower of Cities all!"

WHERE TO GO

There are as many opinions on what is the best way to tour London as there are places to see, but the most efficient method is to start with the major attractions. Once you've hit the highlights and given your camera a good workout, you can then wander along some of the roads less traveled and enjoy a few of the city's subtler charms.

The best way to view London is either by foot or from the top of a double-decker bus. What you lose in time you will make up for in interest. You may spy an unheralded sculpture in a corner of a park, go down a cobblestone alley that hasn't changed in 200 years, or see eye-to-eye with the classical faces on some of the buildings along Piccadilly.

When planning your sightseeing budget, remember that most of the major museums and attractions charge entrance fees, but the British Museum, the National Gallery, the National Portrait Gallery, the Wallace Collection, and the Tate Gallery are notable exceptions (even these, however, charge admission to special exhibitions).

WESTMINSTER AND WHITEHALL

Trafalgar Square and The Mall

To start your tour, go to what must be considered the center of London: **Trafalgar Square.** All distances from London are traditionally measured from Charing Cross, a stone's throw away. There's always something going on around the lion statues and fountains, whether it's pigeons swarming the tourists who bravely fill their hands with birdseed, or the huge public demonstrations in support of an automobile-free central London, or something more politically partisan. The square was named after the naval battle that took place off Cape Trafalgar (south-west Spain) in 1805 in which Admiral Lord Nelson defeated Napoleon. Nelson's statue towers up 52 meters (170 feet) above the square, his shoulders a convenient perch for pigeons.

Grand public buildings like South Africa House, Uganda House, and Canada House face on to the square, but the grandest of all is the **National Gallery,** housing Britain's finest collection of European art. From a group of 38 paintings purchased for the nation in 1824, the National Gallery has grown to include over 2,000 works and is one of the finest collections of Western European art in the world. The collection is divided into four sections: the Sainsbury Wing, the West Wing, the North Wing, and the East Wing. Within each section, the paintings are arranged by school.

To the west of the main building, the Sainsbury Wing (added in 1990), was famously denounced by the Prince of Wales as "a monstrous carbuncle," a bit of an overstatement. This section houses paintings from 1260 to 1510, including Leonardo da Vinci's *Virgin of the Rocks* and Botticelli's *Venus and Mars*.

The West Wing contains paintings from 1510 to 1600, with such greats as Titian's *Bacchus and Ariadne* and Holbein the Younger's *The Ambassadors*. Paintings from 1600 to 1700 are exhibited in the North Wing, where you can admire Rubens's *Le Chapeau de*

Trafalgar Square — a popular hangout for Londoners and visitors alike.

A fairy tale view of London from St. James's Park — the oldest and most charming of the royal parks.

Paille, Rembrandt's *Self Portrait,* and Jan Van Eyck's *Giovanni Arnolfini and his Wife.*

The East Wing, to the right of the main entrance, covers art from 1700 to 1920. Works by the great English painters Constable and Gainsborough are on view here, as are those by Impressionists such as Monet, Van Gogh, Cezanne, and Renoir.

Free hour-long tours of the Gallery are conducted twice daily in winter, three times daily in summer (except Sunday). The Micro Gallery in the Sainsbury Wing houses a computerized information system that allows you to assemble your own tour.

The **National Portrait Gallery** (off Charing Cross, directly behind the National Gallery) was founded in 1856 as a "Gallery of the Portraits of the most eminent persons in British History." Starting at the top of the building, you will see portraits of the medieval worthies, then you can make your way downstairs through royal lineages and historical figures to the 20th century. Such historic Britons as Chaucer, Pepys, and Nell Gwynn, as well as modern notables like

Mick Jagger, the royal family, and Germaine Greer, are all part of the rotating, 9,000-picture collection.

To the east of Trafalgar Square is the fine Baroque church of **St. Martin-in-the-Fields,** a popular venue for free lunchtime concerts, and the model for the old spired churches of New England. Its crypt now houses a café-restaurant and brass-rubbing center, with a fine shop for books, music, and souvenirs. On the south side Admiralty Arch frames a splendid view of **The Mall,** the sweeping boulevard which edges St. James's Park.

St. James's Park is the oldest and most charming of the royal parks, built by Charles II, who wanted to re-create the formal gardens he loved in France, during his exile. One would never guess from its elegant perfection that it was built on the site of a swamp with a leprosarium in the center.

Walk the length of the park from Horse Guards to Buckingham Palace and pause on the bridge in the center of the lake. To the east are the domes and towers of Whitehall, to the west is the Palace — a magical, fairy-tale view either way. The bird sanctuary on Duck Island is home to exotic waterfowl and pelicans (the legacy of a pair presented to Charles II by the Russian ambassador in 1665).

St. James's Palace, on the north side of The Mall shortly before Green Park, was built as a hunting lodge in 1532 by Henry VIII and is now the London home and office of the Prince of Wales. The palace was the official residence of the court before Buckingham Palace took over the role in 1837, and even today all foreign ambassadors are accredited to "The Court of St. James." The public is not admitted, but you can still admire the exterior of this fine Tudor building and have a wander around the charming neighborhood in which it's located.

Along with the Palace of Westminster and the tower of Big Ben, **Buckingham Palace** is a visual symbol of London. It's the townhouse of the Queen, and if the flag is flying above, it means she's at home. The palace was originally built in 1702 for the Duke of Buckingham and was remodeled in 1825 by John Nash. The stately façade is the most recent part of the palace, dating only from 1913. Its architectural stolidity has had countless critics over the years, and its interior is not known for its warmth, but it is a magnificent building nonetheless.

The palace was opened to the public on a limited schedule for the first time in 1993 to help pay for the repairs to the fire-ravaged Windsor Castle and will continue to open during August and September for the foreseeable future. The **Queen's Gallery,** a small modern annex where exhibitions show works of art from the fabulous royal collection, is undergoing substantial renovations and will be reopened in 2002. The remodeling will allow for even more of the Queen's treasures to be viewed. Further up Buckingham

Built in 1702 for the Duke of Buckingham, Buckingham Palace now serves as the townhouse of the Queen.

Palace Road the **Royal Mews** provides opulent stabling for the Queen's horses. You will see what must be the cleanest stables in the world and the ceremonial carriages, including the Glass Coach that carries royal brides to their weddings, and the ornate Gold State Coach that's reserved for coronations and other solemn events.

The Palace of Westminster

There is no place in London that makes one draw in the breath with such appreciation as the **Palace of Westminster** (more commonly known as the Houses of Parliament), the neo-Gothic Victorian triumph on the banks of the Thames. The original palace was built for Edward the Confessor, c. 1065, and for 400 years was a royal residence. The only remaining medieval part of the Palace is Westminster Hall (built 1099). In 1834, someone unwisely decided to dispose of several ancient wooden tally-rods in the basement furnace (Dickens wondered why they weren't instead given to the poor for firewood), and the resulting conflagration soon spread and consumed most of the building. Many considered it a blessing to be able to rebuild the old and drafty edifice. Sir Charles Barry was the driving force behind "this great and

Marvel at the intricate gothic spires of the Palace of Westminster.

beautiful monument to Victorian artifice," completed in 1860. His assistant, Augustus Pugin, provided the inspired Gothic decoration, but literally driven mad by the work, died before its completion.

The public is admitted only to the House of Commons and the House of Lords to hear government debates, although en route to the former you can snatch a glimpse of the splendid medieval interior of Westminster Hall, where Sir Thomas More, Guy Fawkes, and Charles I were all tried and condemned to death. To avoid the lengthy wait for these sessions, British residents should apply well in advance to their particular Member of Parliament and foreign visitors to their embassy in London. Prime Minister's Question Time is on Tuesday and Thursday afternoons in the Commons. Allow plenty of time for the lengthy security process.

From Parliament Square you can see some of the exterior of **Westminster Hall** (to the left of the public entrance to the

The Changing of the Guard

Everyone should see the country's most popular ceremony once. It takes place daily during the summer and on alternate days during winter (wet weather may cause cancellation).

From 11:15 to 11:20am the St. James's Palace part of the Old Guard marches down the Mall to meet the Old Guard of Buckingham Palace. There they await the arrival, at 11:30am, of the New Guard, plus band, from Wellington Barracks (on Birdcage Walk, bordering St. James's Park). The actual change involves the ceremonial handing over of the keys of the Palace and the changing of the sentries at Buckingham Palace and St. James's Palace. Meanwhile the band plays informal tunes. When the change is complete (around 12:05pm) the Old Guard marches back to Wellington Barracks, and the St. James's detachment of the New Guard marches up the Mall to St. James's Palace.

Commons). But more impressive is the river elevation — a counterpoint of pinnacles and spires, the square bulk of the Victoria Tower balanced by the clock tower housing **Big Ben.** The $13^1/2$-ton bell marks the hours with a chime known all over the world. The name is thought to commemorate Sir Benjamin Hall, Chief Commissioner of Works at the time the bell was cast in 1859, but it may also have been named after a popular boxer of the day, one Benjamin Caunt. To really appreciate the magical appeal of these beautiful buildings, take a look from Westminster Bridge on a clear night.

Across the river from Parliament Square is the latest addition to London's skyline, the world's biggest and most technically complex Ferris wheel. Officially known as the **British Airways London Eye,** it's 135 meters (443 feet) high, weighs 1,600 tons, and has a circumference of 424 meters (1,392 feet). Although it did not start running as planned on the eve of the millennium — having failed a final inspection — once operational, the London Eye will take up to 800 passengers on a 30-minute ride that comes complete with running commentary on the sights of London spreading out below.

The **Tate Gallery,** on the river at Millbank, a short walk south from Parliament Square, houses the National Collection of British Historic Painting (dating from the 16th century). Some of the highlights of the collection include Constable's famous views of Salisbury Cathedral, Joshua Reynold's portraits, Hogarth's acerbic commentaries on 18th-century low life, Stubbs's landscape and sporting scenes, Gainsborough's portraits and naturalistic landscapes, and the romantic epics of the pre-Raphaelite Group. The Clore Gallery (an extension of the main building) was built to hold the huge Turner catalogue, which includes 282 oil paintings and more than 20,000 other works by the Covent Garden–born artist.

Westminster Abbey

Westminster Abbey is Britain's coronation church, a royal mausoleum, and a national shrine. Kings and queens lie buried here alongside eminent statesmen, soldiers, scientists, musicians, and men of letters. The High Altar has been the scene of every coronation for the last 900 years — as well as many royal weddings. But the Abbey remains a house of worship with services taking place on Sundays, when the highly acclaimed Westminster Boys' School Choir sings.

The towering home of Big Ben — London's most famous landmark.

The nave is open daily, free of charge, but you have to pay to go beyond the screen where the Royal Chapels, Poets' Corner, and other areas of interest lie (closed on Sunday). Regular Abbey "Supertours" are conducted by vergers, who can reveal some of the hidden wonders of this ancient church. Go to the information desk in the nave for details.

The West Door leads directly into the nave, which soars to a height of nearly 31 meters (102 feet). The first grave that you will pass is the **Tomb of the Unknown Warrior.** It is a great irony that here among so many great statesmen and members of royalty the most visited tomb is that of an unknown soldier. It is the only floor tomb in the nave upon which it is forbidden to tread; even royal processions detour around it. During the

A skyward glimpse of the 13th-century Chapter House ceiling at the glorious Westminster Abbey.

week of Remembrance Day, when the whole nation falls silent for two minutes at the eleventh hour of the eleventh day of the eleventh month, the forecourts of the Abbey are alive with red poppies and temporary memorials to those who have gone down in battle, even fallen animals.

Beyond the screen is **Statesmen's Corner,** where many British Prime Ministers are buried, including Gladstone. The royal tombs lie around the **High Altar.** Moving counter-clockwise you will see the final resting places of Edward I, Henry III, Edward III, and Richard II. In the center of the Altar is the **Coronation Chair,** a great, battered oaken throne used for the crowning of every monarch since 1307.

Further into the church the **Chapel of Henry VII** is breathtaking, ablaze with the banners and pennants of the Order of the Knights of the Bath (an old chivalric order), adorned with intricately carved wood and masonry, the stone fan vaulting above as delicate as lace. Henry commissioned this masterpiece in 1503 to serve as his final resting-place.

Around the chapel (moving counter-clockwise) are buried: Elizabeth I and ("Bloody") Mary I — sisters, but with an extremely uneasy relationship — Mary imprisoned Elizabeth in the Tower and came very close to having her executed; Henry VII; the Stuart Monarchs — a vault holding Charles II and William III as well as Mary Queen of Scots.

Walk back past the High Altar to **Poets' Corner** where Chaucer, Spenser, Dickens, Hardy, Kipling, and Browning are buried (playwright Ben Jonson was buried standing up to save space). There are various memorials to almost every literary figure in the Britain, although most of them are actually buried elsewhere, and many were memorialized long after they died. The actor Sir Laurence Olivier was the last person buried in Poet's Corner, which was finally declared full and closed for business in 1989.

A side exit takes you to the **Great Cloister** area, which includes the octagonal **Chapter House,** where Parliament once sat, as well as the ancient **Chapel of the Pyx** and the **Abbey Treasures Museum.** A single ticket covers admission to all three.

Seats of Power

Whitehall is the area of government buildings that extends from Parliament Square to Trafalgar Square. The name comes from Henry VIII's Palace of Whitehall, of which the Banqueting House is all that now survives.

Heading along Parliament Street from Bridge Street, you pass the imposing late-19th-century headquarters of the Treasury. Some 3 meters (10 feet) underground sprawl the once hidden **Cabinet War Rooms,** Churchill's command post during the war years (entrance at Clive Steps in King Charles

Street off Whitehall; Tel. 0207/930-6961), which can be visited daily from 10am to 6pm for an admission charge.

Just a few yards away is **Number 10 Downing Street,** office and residence of the prime minister since 1735. The unimposing Number 10 can be glimpsed from the street, but without the police officer outside the front door, you'd never know this house tucked away behind gates was of any great importance.

Parliament for a New Millennium

For 800 years, England's Parliament has been in the somewhat contradictory business of maintaining a democratic, representative government while retaining the feudal practice of hereditary peers sitting in the House of Lords. In 1999, this anachronism was up-ended, and the process of modernizing the Houses of Parliament began in earnest. The Houses of Parliament are divided into Commons (elected representatives) and Lords, who are either life peers (people appointed to the post by the Queen or the government) or first-born sons of the nobility. The fact that this second chamber of the Houses of Parliament was based on such an absurd qualification (you wouldn't choose a dog that way, Lloyd George said in 1910) and could serve a lifetime has always caused disgruntlement among some people, especially among the elected members of government. The Labor government gave the House of Lords the order to abolish the hereditary peers in 1999. The Lords were allowed to elect 92 of the hereditary lords to remain in the house, but the other 555 peers in Parliament lost their membership in that exclusive club. A tradition of 800 years finally fell under the ax, and the remaining 92 hereditary lords are in no way secure in their jobs. The life peers will presumably remain. The future of the House of Lords is a mystery, apparently even to the government making the changes. As one of the Lords said upon leaving his seat, "It would appear that Guy Fawkes had a more coherent plan than these people."

Parliament Street becomes Whitehall at the junction with the Cenotaph, the monolithic memorial commemorating the dead of the two World Wars. A little farther on is the **Banqueting House,** built in 1619 by Inigo Jones for James I as England's first truly Renaissance building, inspired by Jones's hero, the 16th-century Italian master Palladio. Its major feature is a splendid ceiling by Rubens, commissioned by Charles I. It was in front of this building that Charles I was beheaded in 1649.

The ghostly detail of Rodin's "Burghers of Calais" in front of the Palace of Westminster.

The **Horse Guards,** on the west side of Whitehall, duly maintain their traditional sentry posts, as this is still the official entry to the royal palaces, even though Whitehall burned down in 1698 and St. James's Palace has long ceased to be the main royal residence.

A guard-change ceremony takes place Monday to Saturday at 11am and on Sunday at 10am, and an inspection is carried out at 4pm. Through the gates lies the Horse Guards' Parade, scene in June of "Beating the Retreat" and "Trooping the Color" (see Calendar of Events on page 91).

Along the Strand

The Strand links Westminster to the City along a route opened in Edward the Confessor's time. It was along this road that

Eleanor of Castile's body was carried in 1293, with twelve crosses erected along the way, one of which was Charing Cross. Today it is a street of shops and theaters, with the occasional beauty along the way such as the world famous Savoy Hotel, in front of which is the only British road where traffic drives on the right side of the street.

On the Embankment stands Cleopatra's Needle, the city's oldest outdoor monument.

The classical church of **St. Mary-le-Strand,** built in 1724, originally stood on the north side of the street; upon the advent of the motor car, the church was left in place as the road was widened, leaving it an island stranded in mid-Strand in the churning traffic.

The **Courtauld Institute Galleries** at Somerset House provide a superb crash course in art history. The collection features 14th-, 15th-, and 16th-century religious masterpieces, 17th-century Italian art, 20th-century British art, and key works by Rubens, Cranach, Brueghel, and Botticelli. However, the two rooms, into which most people crowd, house the Impressionists and Post-Impressionists. Here you will find Manet's *Bar at the Folies-Bergère* and a sketch for *Déjeuner sur l'Herbe*; *La Loge* by Renoir; Van Gogh's *Self-Portrait with Bandaged Ear;* and *Nevermore* by Gauguin.

Down on the Embankment, parallel to the Strand, the traffic is still heavy, but there are riverside views. Here, too, you will find London's oldest outdoor monument, a 21-meter (68-foot) Egyptian obelisk, called **Cleopatra's Needle,** cut from the quarries of Aswan (c. 1475 B.C.). It was one of a pair — the other one stands in Central Park in New York City — and was given to the Empire by the Turkish Viceroy of Egypt in 1819, yet it took 59 years for the British to get it from where it lay in the sand to its present position — not the best for such a treasure, but the planned site in front of the Houses of Parliament turned out to be unstable. The sphinxes at the base were apparently placed facing the wrong direction.

Away across the river near Waterloo Bridge is the **South Bank Arts Centre.** This is the home of the Hayward Gallery, the National Theatre, the Royal Festival Hall, and the National Film Theatre. The brutalist architecture and worn-out exterior is particularly unattractive, but it is nevertheless functional. Plans are afoot to improve its looks in the new century.

THE CITY

While in the past the City was London proper, where citizens lived, worked and played, the ever-expanding nature of the city pushed its boundaries outwards, and the Blitz dealt a real blow to its intimate ancient design. Where once markets flourished and coffeehouses percolated with wheeling and dealing, now soul-less skyscrapers and one-way streets prevail. You'll still find incongruous remnants of the old City — narrow lanes and alleyways that will remind you what the medieval street pattern must have looked like. But the only way to see the City is on foot, otherwise you may miss these echoes of the past.

Nowadays, the City (short for the City of London) takes care of business. Five days a week, over 300,000 commuters pour into the area known as "the Square Mile" and busy themselves with every kind of financial activity known to man. At

5 or 6pm they pour back out again, leaving a comparative ghost town of some 6,000 residents. Forget weekends…you must visit the City during office hours when the area is alive and pubs and restaurants are in full swing. Amazingly, even most of the churches in the City close on Sunday.

The Square Mile extends from the Law Courts (at the junction of the Strand and Fleet Street) on the west to the Tower of London on the east, and from the Barbican in the north to the Thames on the south. This was the area originally enclosed by the Roman Wall, but is now firmly held in place by commerce.

Legal London

Legal London starts at the very edge of the city with the **Royal Courts of Justice** (better known as the Law Courts), located in a late 19th-century building on the Strand that looks more like a fairy-tale castle than the home of English civil law. On the other side of busy Fleet Street a few yards down, a tiny alleyway leads to the gas-lit sanctuary of the area known as the

Wren's Prodigious Output

In 1663 Christopher Wren was asked to make repairs to Old St. Paul's Cathedral, which had stood for over 500 years. He recommended that it should be completely remodeled, but this suggestion was rejected. However, the Great Fire of 1666 paved the way for something even more drastic, namely a totally new cathedral. Although his only engineering resources were manpower and pulleys, Parliament was nonetheless exasperated by the slow rate of progress and halved his already meager salary of £200 to £100 per annum. During this time he was also engaged in the design of 53 churches, The Royal Hospital at Chelsea, The Monument, Hampton Court Palace, St. James's Palace, and the Royal Naval Hospital at Greenwich.

The Royal Courts of Justice, the home of English civil law, is a fine example of London's rich architectural heritage.

Temple, which houses two of the four **Inns of Court** — Inner Temple and Middle Temple. In former times they were the residences of barristers and barristers-in-training. Even today barristers-in-training must be members of an Inn.

The Temple itself takes its name from its 12th- and 13th-century function as the home of the crusading Knights Templar. Visitors have access to the round Temple church, built in 1185. The magnificent 16th-century Middle Temple Hall is open to the public Monday through Friday from 10 to 11:30am and 3 to 4pm if not in use.

Walk up Chancery Lane, to the ancient gatehouse of Lincoln's Inn, above which Oliver Cromwell once studied. **Lincoln's Inn** has legal records dating back to 1422, making it the oldest of the four Inns of Court. The Old Hall in front dates back to 1490 and the adjacent New Buildings are only new by the Inn's standards, dating back some 300 years. The gardens here are particularly beautiful and are open Monday through Friday from noon to 2:30pm.

North of Lincoln's Inn, on the large public square known as Lincoln's Inn fields, is **Sir John Soane's Museum,** which holds several famous Hogarth paintings (including *The Rake's Progress* series) plus works by Turner and Canaletto. Soane was a prominent late 18th-century London architect and his fascinating house has been kept precisely how he left it.

Make your way back down along Chancery Lane (or Fetter Lane) and turn left onto Fleet Street, where you can visit **Dr. Samuel Johnson's House** in Gough Square. It was here that the first definitive English dictionary was compiled. Although Johnson's favorite watering hole was the Wine Office Court, he may have, in a pinch, resorted to **Ye Olde**

Completed in 1710, the St. Paul's Cathedral testifies to the brilliance of its designer, Sir Christopher Wren.

Cheshire Cheese. Dickens also drank here, and so little has changed that both he and Johnson might still feel at home, although certainly appalled by all the tourists.

St. Paul's Cathedral

Christopher Wren was not only the first architect to super-vise the construction of an English cathedral single-handed, but he also had the rare good fortune to live long enough to see his dream realized and is even buried in the crypt of St. Paul's. On the simple tomb, Wren's son wrote the Latin epi-taph which translates: "Reader, if you seek his monument, look around you."

Balance and clarity distinguish Wren's design. The interior can only be described as awesome. Among the most out-standing elements are Grinling Gibbons's beautifully carved choir stalls, Jean Tijou's wrought-iron choir screen and gates, and, of course, the dome itself. This is the second largest in the world (after St. Peter's in Rome), rising to 111 meters (365 feet). Climb up to the first level, to experience the freak acoustics of the **Whispering Gallery** where you can clearly hear someone softly murmur from 33 meters (107 feet) away. A total of 627 steps ascend to the very top for dizzying views of the City.

Westminster Abbey may hold the royal remains, but there are also many famous monuments and tombs in St. Paul's. The most notable are those to the Duke of Wellington and Admiral Lord Nelson. Don't miss the **statue of John Donne** rescued from the ruins of Old St. Paul's Cathedral. The great poet was Dean of the cathedral, and his likeness, wrapped in a funeral shroud, is scorch-marked, a legacy from the Great Fire.

As must be appropriate for a church that has seen use as a commercial market and meeting place, with wrestling, ball-playing, horse-trading, and worse going on, there is a cash register at the entrance to the Cathedral, and a rather stiff charge to enter. On Sunday the cathedral is open for services only.

The Barbican

A concrete jungle to the north of the City is home to the **Barbican Arts and Conference Centre**. As with the South Bank complex, its architecture has won few friends, but here too the cultural offerings are excellent, and include picture galleries, theaters, a cinema, bars, and restaurants. It is also the London home of the Royal Shakespeare Company and the London Symphony Orchestra. Go along at lunchtime for free foyer concerts.

The other pride of the Barbican Centre (just outside the Arts Centre) is the excellent **Museum of London** (London Wall, the Barbican). The well-presented modern galleries chart every aspect of the capital from its beginnings as *Londinium* to the present. From Roman times, to the Blitz, to the building of the Millennium Dome, the museum offers the kind of artifacts that make history come alive. A Roman kitchen and a section of a Roman Wall, a plague bell, the old door of Newgate Prison, the Lord Mayor's gilded State Coach, a Victorian grocery store, an elevator from Selfridges, and an Anderson shelter from the Blitz are just some of the fascinating recreations and exhibits found there.

The Financial City

The heart of the business district of the City focuses on the **Bank of England** (nicknamed "The Old Lady of Threadneedle Street"). Imposing windowless walls rise impregnably, with seven stories above ground and three below. This is where the nation's gold reserves are kept. The bank no longer deals with the general public, but there is a small, free museum (entrance on Bartholomew Lane; open Mon–Fri

10am–5pm) that tells the story of English currency and of the Bank itself, which has weathered a few storms in its day.

The tower block next door to the Bank of England is the **Stock Exchange** building, and the splendid classical structure just across the road is the **Royal Exchange,** built in 1844. Opposite the Bank of England is another classical-style building, the 18th-century **Mansion House,** official residence of the Lord Mayor of London during his or her year of office (open to group tours only).

Next to Mansion House is possibly the finest of Wren's City churches, **St. Stephen Walbrook.** Its lovely dome is said to have been a rehearsal for the larger cupola of St. Paul's, and the interior was restored from 1978 to 1987.

Due east of the Bank of England, along the ancient thoroughfares of Cornhill and Leadenhall Street, is **Lloyd's of London.** Lloyd's originated in 1688 in Edward Lloyd's Coffee House, where ships' captains, merchants, and ship

Down in the heart of London's business district, you'll find the stately Royal Exchange building, built in 1844.

owners would gather to exchange news and carry out marine insurance deals. Lloyd's moved to the space-age building designed by Richard Rogers in 1986. A huge atrium rises 61 meters (200 feet) at the heart of this steel and glass structure which, like Rogers's Pompidou Centre in Paris, exposes everything to view. Only pre-booked groups are admitted to the building, which contains a small museum.

In the shadow of Lloyd's, the Victorian cast iron and glass of **Leadenhall Market** is altogether more down to earth and also more atmospheric. The quality of the fruit, vegetables, and poultry have been enticing City dwellers here since the Middle Ages, although prices were probably a lot better then.

Just south of here, **The Monument** (Monument Street) raises its flaming urn in memory of the Great Fire of London in 1666, which swept away the medieval City. The Monument towers 61 meters (202 feet) high, the exact distance due east to the site of the baker's shop in Pudding Lane

From royal palace, to prison, to place of execution — the Tower of London has worn many hats in its 900 years.

where the fire started. It's a magnificent view, which should not be missed by those who don't suffer from vertigo (open daily 10am–6pm; adult £1.50, child 50p.).

Northwest of the Bank of England, along Princes Street and Gresham Street, is the **Guildhall** (King Street), the town hall of the City. This resilient building dates from 1411 and has withstood the Great Fire and the Blitz. Step inside (during office hours) for a free look at the ancient Great Hall. Here the functions and ceremonies of the City of London carry on today as they have for centuries: banquets of state, the annual swearing-in of the new mayor in November, and every third Thursday (except in August) meetings of the Court of Common Council. The banners of the twelve principal City Livery Companies (craft guilds whose members once wore a distinct livery) hang around the Hall. In total there are 94 Livery companies and their members elect the Lord Mayor.

Around the Tower

The **Tower of London** is London's greatest historical sight. Throughout its 900-year history it has been a fortress, a royal palace, a notorious prison, and place of execution.

Grim though its history is, the Tower looks benign enough today, surrounded by pleasant green lawns in the moat that the Duke of Wellington had filled in for sanitation reasons in the 19th century. (There are plans to fill it with water again in the near future.) Stormed by over two million visitors a year, the fortifications are manned by 41 Yeomen Warders. Known as "Beefeaters," these ex-military men dress in Tudor costume and give continuous free introductory tours, which are both informative and entertaining. If you want to beat the crowds, arrive early. Note that each February the Crown Jewels are closed to the public, and there is a reduced entry charge to the Tower.

Enjoy a marvelous panoramic view of the Thames from atop Tower Bridge.

Your tour will pass by the **Traitors' Gate,** which was the river entrance to the Tower before the Thames was moved back. Those accused of treason were brought here by boat, as was the future Queen Elizabeth I, following in the footsteps of her tragic mother, Anne Boleyn. Above the gate is Edward I's Palace, home to the King in the late 13th century and the only surviving medieval palace in England. The **Bloody Tower** (opposite) takes its name from one of the most dire deeds in British history. The "Little Princes," Edward and Richard, were interred here in 1483 by their uncle, Richard of Gloucester (later Richard III), and were never to be seen again — though two centuries later two small skeletons were discovered nearby. Another famous occupant was Sir Walter Raleigh, who was sent here for allegedly conspiring against King James I. Raleigh's Walk commemorates his restless daily constitutionals.

Tower Green is the site of the execution block where six noble persons are known to have lost their heads. These include two of Henry VIII's wives, Anne Boleyn and Catherine Howard, and the "nine-day Queen" Lady Jane Grey. Commoners, including Sir Thomas More, were executed in public outside the Tower walls on Tower Hill, in front of crowds of up to 200,000 people.

After visiting the beautiful, though melancholy, chapel of **St. Peter ad Vincula,** where lie the headless bodies of many famous execution victims, you may want to see the **Crown Jewels.** The royal regalia date largely from the Restoration of Charles II in 1660. The Crown of St. Edward, named after the Confessor, was made for the coronation of Charles II and has been used at every coronation since. It is so heavy at 2 kilograms (5 pounds) that it is exchanged at the first opportunity for the Imperial State Crown. Studded with some 3,250 jewels, this holds the Black Prince's ruby and the Second Star of Africa.

Many of the pieces of armor in the **Royal Armouries** in the White Tower have been moved to a larger museum in Leeds, but what remain are the historical items that relate directly to the Tower, such as Henry VIII's huge suit of armor, and Charles I's considerably smaller outfit. The **White Tower** itself is the oldest part of the Tower of London, and the **Chapel of St. John** dates from 1080.

Look into the Wakefield Tower, where Henry VI was murdered, and stroll along the **Wall Walk,** where prisoners were allowed to take the air. Look out, too, for the Tower ravens; according to legend, if the ravens ever leave, the Tower and England will fall. New ravens are bred and their wings are clipped to ensure that they will stay. There is a remarkable raven there now, named Thor, who has been taught to imitate human speech.

Below the Tower is **Tower Bridge,** one of London's most famous landmarks. This marvel of Victorian engineering, clad in Gothic-style stonework, matches the Tower in appearance. Overhead walkways provide magnificent panoramic views up and down the river. Exhibits illustrating the history of the bridge can be seen at the Tower Bridge Museum.

Moored opposite the Tower on the south bank of the river, the **_H.M.S. Belfast_** (Morgan's Lane, Tooley Street; Tel. 0207/940 6328) last saw action in World War II and Korea.

You can take a ferry from Tower Pier and look over the entire ship to gain an insight into the difficult conditions of war at sea, though the museum is as enlightening about life at sea during peacetime as during war. It is open from March through October 10am to 6pm; there is an admission charge.

The innovative and ambitious **Design Museum** (at the far end of Butler's Wharf, east of Tower Bridge; Tel. 0207/403 6933) features the very latest designs that mass production has to offer, some still on the drawing board, others already in production. In more traditional museum fashion, exhibits chronicling the development of the design of such familiar household items as the telephone or vacuum cleaner are surprisingly interesting. Hours are 11:30am to 6pm Monday to Saturday; there is an admission charge.

THE WEST END

Despite its name, the West End is really the center of town and hardly the end of London at all. It's where you'll find the theaters, nightclubs, major stores, smart hotels, and many of the best restaurants. Oxford Street and Piccadilly are the most famous streets and form the approximate north–south boundaries of the West End. This also takes in the central neighborhoods of Mayfair, Soho, St. James's, and Covent Garden.

Piccadilly

West End sightseeing usually starts at **Piccadilly Circus,** where neon lights have shone brightly for more than a century. The celebrated traffic circle (the meaning of *circus*) has been pedestrianized and is a popular hangout for tourists and buskers. Piccadilly Circus is absurdly loud and busy at night and on weekends. There's a lot to see: Segaworld, a huge futuristic indoor theme park; the enormous Tower records, and Madame Tussauds Rock Circus are all there.

The famous statue of **Eros** was reviled when it was erected in 1893. Dedicated to a philanthropist, the Earl of Shaftesbury, it was intended to represent the Angel of Christian Charity, and not, as it has become known, Eros, the Greek God of sexual love. It was also supposed to be facing up Shaftsbury Avenue, but over the years it has been moved so often — it spent the second world war in Surrey — it's amazing that the statue is only slightly askew. The statue so offended the Victorians that it could have been removed without protest when it was first unveiled, but it has certainly grown to be one of the great symbols of London.

Just a few yards away is **Leicester Square** (pronounced "Lester"), another insanely crowded meeting place, where the big West End cinemas feature first-run blockbusters. Here you'll also find nightclubs and the Society of West End Theatre (SWET) half-price ticket booth (see page 87). It has

Bright lights, big city — atop Piccadilly Circus, London's equivalent to New York City's Time's Square.

street artists, musicians, and the occasional carnival, and should be avoided on weekends if you can't stand mobs.

Piccadilly (the street) links Piccadilly Circus to Hyde Park Corner. In the midst of a mile-long stretch of airline offices, shops, and hotels, the square brick tower of **St. James's Church, Piccadilly,** signals a charming oasis. This church is considered one of Wren's best — and it is home to a number of daily markets selling crafts and antiques, and has a café too.

Across the street is 17th-century Burlington House, home of the **Royal Academy of Arts,** which has been London's most prestigious exhibition space for almost three centuries and regularly shows exhibitions of international fame. Its temporary exhibitions and annual Summer Exhibition of contemporary artists draw enormous crowds. The Monet exhibit of 1999 was so wildly popular that the Academy resorted to 24-hour opening times to accommodate the ticket holders.

Alongside the Royal Academy is **Burlington Arcade,** one of the oldest and most elegant of the capital's covered shopping promenades, built in 1815.

Fortnum and Mason (181 Piccadilly) is another Piccadilly institution, and a very grand grocery store. Afternoon tea at Fortnum's is a must for the out-of-towner. Or, if Fortnum's is too crowded,

The Albert Memorial — in memory of Queen Victoria's beloved consort.

there's always the **Ritz** (150 Piccadilly). Be warned, though: Getting a reservation for afternoon tea here can be difficult, and getting into the hotel in jeans and sneakers is impossible. The Ritz backs on to Green Park, the smallest of the royal parks, and the only one without flower beds, hence the name.

Piccadilly ends at Hyde Park Corner. Facing Wellington Arch (also called Constitution Arch) is **Apsley House** (141 Piccadilly; Tel. 0207/499-5676), which was styled rather pretentiously as No. 1, London. This is the former residence of the Duke of Wellington, and is now home to the Wellington Museum. There's a very fine collection of paintings by several Old Masters, a bizarre statue of Wellington's closest enemy Napoleon, and a magnificent silver table centerpiece. The views from the windows of the park are a rare and beautiful sight. The museum is open Tuesday through Sunday from 11am to 5pm; there is an admission charge.

Hyde Park is probably the best known of the royal parks due to its central location, its size (138 hectares/340 acres) and its visitor attractions. At the Marble Arch corner of the park is **Speakers' Corner.** Historically, this is the point where mass demonstrations used to take place, and the right of free assembly was guaranteed here. Sunday morning is when soapbox orators spout their stuff, which has come to be disappointingly focused on religious fundamentalism rather than political or philosophical issues.

When you tire of lending your ears, take a boat out on the **Serpentine,** Hyde Park's artificial lake, or take the plunge in the Lido, the part of the Serpentine reserved for hardy swimmers. You will notice a small island in the Serpentine, and can only surmise that nearby resident J.M. Barrie imagined it as the Island of the Lost Boys. The beloved statue of his famous creation Peter Pan stands eternally looking across the lake. Across West Carriage Drive is Kensington Gardens (see page 62), where you will find temporary exhibitions of modern art at the **Serpentine Gallery** (Tel. 0207/402 6075).

The **Albert Memorial,** recently restored to its former glory, can be seen from all over Hyde Park and Kensington Gardens. It commemorates Queen Victoria's beloved consort, whose early death she mourned for nearly forty years. In front of the memorial is where daredevil in-line skaters flaunt their talents. Across the street is the domed Albert Hall.

Mayfair

Mayfair lies to the north of Piccadilly, between Park Lane and Regent Street. Some of the city's most elegant shops and exclusive clubs are to be found here. But Mayfair wasn't always so grand. The name recalls the boisterous May Fair, held at Shepherd Market during the late 17th and early 18th centuries and home to prostitution, drinking, brawling, and crimes of every stripe. It was finally banned forever by disgusted officials.

Bond Street has an amazing collection of very expensive shops. Cashmere, jewelry, Old Master paintings, and fine antiques are the stock in trade here. The presence of **Sotheby's** (34 Bond St.), the world's oldest firm of art auctioneers, says much about the street. Running north from here, Savile Row outfits Britain's — and some of the world's — best-dressed men. Large luxury hotels line Park Lane, no longer a lane now, but a boulevard with bumper-to-bumper traffic, day and night.

Marble Arch, at the top of Park Lane, is the gateway to Oxford Street, but the area used to be the gateway to hell: Between 1388 and 1783 this was the capital's place of public execution. In 1571 the notorious Tyburn Tree, a triangular scaffold on which 24 people at one time could be hanged, was erected here. Horribly, it was a favorite London pastime to go watch the hangings.

Famous figures such as Henry VIII and two of his six wives are eerily immortalized at Madame Tussauds.

The monumental **Marble Arch** was designed by John Nash to celebrate the victories of Trafalgar and Waterloo, and was originally erected in front of Buckingham Palace in 1827. Nash was working on the design of the Palace, but owing to budget overruns he was dismissed, and in 1851 his Marble Arch was moved to its present, somewhat ludicrous site.

The **Wallace Collection** (at Hertford House, Manchester Square) is an enticing (and free) attraction that is a rare combination of stately home, art gallery, and museum. It features 18th-century French furniture (with pieces from Marie Antoinette's apartments at Versailles), exquisite Sèvres porcelain, and paintings by Watteau, Fragonard, and Boucher. Alongside works by Rembrandt, Titian, Velázquez, and Rubens sits one of the world's favorite paintings, the *Laughing Cavalier* by Frans Hals.

Run the gauntlet of **Oxford Street** if you're in the mood for serious shopping in big stores and chain shops. Regent

Street is a bit more interesting. Here you will find **Liberty,** for fabulous floral fabrics; **Hamleys,** a six-floor toy emporium; and **Garrard,** "the Crown Jeweller."

Baker Street was made famous by Arthur Conan Doyle and his character Sherlock Holmes, whose legendary residence is commemorated by the **Sherlock Holmes Museum** (221B Baker St., Tel. 0207/935 8866), a charming if overpriced attraction. It is open daily from 10am to 6pm.

Nearby is one of the most popular attractions in London. Despite the horrific lines and the questionable value, **Madame Tussauds,** keeps packing in the tourists, as it has been doing at the present site on Marylebone Road since 1884. The corniness of the celebrity wax figures is slightly offset by the genuinely chilling scenes in the Chamber of Horrors. A combined ticket is available for the London Planetarium next door, which shows a film on its dome and has a few space-related exhibits.

If Madame Tussauds has got you a bit perturbed — escape to the lush elegance of central London's Regent's Park.

If you would like a break from the crowds and some fresh air after visiting Madame Tussauds, take the short stroll to **Regent's Park.** The elegant white stucco buildings bordering the park were designed by the Prince Regent's architect, John Nash, and laid out during the 1820s. Despite the failure of Nash's grand plan for the area, what remains is undoubtedly the most elegant example of town planning in central London. None of the park's buildings are open to the public, but some of their exteriors are the finest in London — don't miss Cumberland Terrace.

The park's **Open-Air Theater** is a delightful place to watch Shakespeare under the stars on a balmy summer evening. If you would like to reach the park by water, narrow boats ply the Regent's Canal from Little Venice (by Warwick Avenue underground station) and are a very pleasant way to travel to the park on a fine day.

St. James's

Officers and gentlemen frequent St. James's, the area south of Piccadilly. Here in the heart of clubland (gentlemen's clubs, not nightclubs) you will find centuries-old wine merchants, hatters, shirtmakers, and shoemakers who cater for the most discerning masculine tastes.

The famous **clubs,** beloved of Jules Verne's Phileas Fogg, Beau Brummell, and other 18th-century gentlemen, line Pall Mall and St. James's Street. Don't look for signs, though, announcing any names, as discreet anonymity is the watchword. Today, there are fewer than thirty clubs, but St. James's is still an upper-class male bastion.

Christie's auctioneers, at 8 King St., has been Sotheby's rival since 1766.

Some of the shops in this area resemble time capsules, like historic re-creations in museum. You can order a top hat from

James Lock (est. 1759), handmade shoes from **John Lobb** (est. 1849), or vintage wines from **Berry Bros and Rudd** (est. 1699). Have a look in their windows at the very least: Lobb displays a pair of moccasin-boots given in the 19th-century by a Native American princess from Minnesota.

The area derives its name from **St. James's Palace,** which stands between Pall Mall and The Mall (see page 26). At the end of Pall Mall is the **Duke of York's Column,** a memorial to George III's impecunious son, who was the Commander-in-Chief of the British Forces. The Duke died with debts of over £2 million, and the statue was paid for by withholding one day's pay from every officer and soldier. This unpopular measure helped condemn his memory; the nursery rhyme about the "Grand Old Duke of York" who marched his men to the top of the hill and then back down for no apparent reason was a satirical comment on his indecisive nature.

Soho

The popular image of Soho (the word comes from an old hunting cry) as a seedy red-light district is fast becoming outdated. There are still prostitutes and there are still sex shows, but by international standards Soho is safe for the casual visitor. Nowadays it is better known for its vast choice of international restaurants.

Its cosmopolitan make-up dates back to an influx of Huguenot and Greek refugees in the 17th century. Soho soon became a melting pot for many European nationalities, and most recently a significant Chinese community. Atmospheric Old Compton Street is a good example of the area's multinational flavor, with an Algerian coffee shop, an Italian delicatessen, and restaurants representing France, Italy, Malaysia, Vietnam, and the United States. Pâtisserie Valerie on this street is one of London's favorite teashops. The street is also the center of Soho's gay community.

Chinatown is a tiny district center that centers around Gerrard Street. Street names here are subtitled in Chinese, and the tops of telephone boxes resemble mini pagodas. Eating out is the major attraction. At the eastern edge of Soho is **Charing Cross Road,** the center of London's antiquarian book trade, with many charming, dusty old second-book stores.

Enter the dragon — duck into Soho's Chinatown for some unforgettable dim sum.

Covent Garden

Covent Garden's name is a corruption of "convent garden," a reminder that before the Dissolution of the Monasteries this land was cultivated by the monks of Westminster Abbey. Developed with patrician townhouses in the 17th century, Covent Garden became a bohemian area of pubs and coffeehouses, popular with writers and artists. Rather like its neighbor, Soho, it was definitely seedy, and, at times, downright dangerous. It is no coincidence that London's first police force was established here in Bow Street.

A market for fruit and vegetables was set up in the 17th century and so thrived for over two centuries that the permanent **Central Market Halls** were built in the mid–19th century. However, traffic congestion finally meant the departure of the market to South London in 1974 and the redevelop-

The endless rows of trendy shops, stands, cafés, and more draw a constant drove of crowds to Covent Garden.

ment of Covent Garden. Since then all kinds of trendy shops, markets, restaurants, bars, and museums have been attracted to the area, most of which stay open late seven days a week.

Inigo Jones' striking **St. Paul's Church** holds down the west side of the piazza, and it is in front of here that London's very best buskers entertain.

The old Flower Market hall to the east accommodates the charming **London Transport Museum,** which is a delight for both young (for hands-on fun) and old (for nostalgia). You can see London's first, horse-drawn omnibus and some of the world's first underground carriages and trains. A simulator allows you to take the driving seat in an underground train along the Circle line.

The **Theatre Museum,** next door, is one of London's unsung treasures, reflecting that "the Garden" is at the heart of the performing arts in London. Dedicated to all aspects of the performing arts, it has a marvelous array of props, stage models, costumes, prints, and posters.

Indeed, in this neighborhood you'll find plenty of theaters, and the world-famous **Royal Opera House,** home of the Royal Opera and Royal Ballet companies. Backstage tours are given at the Theatre Royal in Drury Lane.

Take time out to wander the tiny alleyways, particularly the charming, gas-lit **Goodwin's Court,** which connects St. Martin's Lane to Bedfordbury. The lovely bow-windowed houses date from the late 18th century. Health-conscious eaters should head for **Neal's Yard,** hidden away off Neal Street. A bakery, an herbal apothecary, cafés, and food shops cluster round a quaint cobbled courtyard.

Bloomsbury

London's most erudite district is heavily associated with the early 20th-century literary life of the Bloomsbury Group, an association of artists and writers including E.M. Forster, Virginia Woolf, and Roger Fry. The neighborhood is characterized by several charming squares, where blue plaques mark the many homes of the famous. The British Museum and the University of London are the heart and soul of this area.

The splendid **British Museum** on Great Russell Street opened to the public in 1759, although the present building dates from 1823. Within its 7 hectares (17½ acres) it holds one of the largest and finest collections of antiquities in the world, magnificent medieval treasures, and many of the world's oldest and most famous documents and books. Extensive as the museum is, its collections are continually expanding — a recent addition is the Weston Gallery of Roman Britain, documenting 400 years of Roman occupation.

For an introduction to the collection take one of the museum's own guided tours — even the most up-to-date guidebook will not be able to keep up with the recent changes in

The British Museum houses one of the world's finest collection of antiquities.

the museum. Because of the construction of an enclosed courtyard with the famed **Reading Room** at the center, the collection will be moved around quite a bit.

Be sure to find the following treasures, which are the jewels in this magnificent museum's crown:

The **Assyrian Sculptures and Reliefs — The Khorsabad Entrance** form the colossal gateway from 710 B.C. complete with huge, human-headed winged bulls and magnificent stone panels depicting hunting scenes

The **Elgin Marbles** are the friezes and figures from the Parthenon in Athens, whose ownership is still a hotly contested issue between Greece and England.

The **Rosetta Stone,** discovered by Napoleon's army, was the first key to deciphering hieroglyphics.

Within the rooms devoted to **Egyptian Mummies,** there are not only mummified humans, but also sacred mummified animals, which range vastly in size from a shrew to a small bull.

The **Sutton Hoo Treasure** is from the burial ship of an ancient English king, dating from around A.D. 625, and found at Sutton Hoo in Suffolk in 1939.

Other areas with great and popular treasures include the Mausoleum of Halicarnassus, the Manuscript Saloon, the Babylonian Room, Prints and Drawings, Celtic Britain,

Roman Britain, the Medieval Gallery, Clocks and Watches, and the Portland Vase.

Almost a century before the Bloomsbury Group moved in, Charles Dickens lived and worked at 48 Doughty Street, and his home is now the **Dickens's House Museum** (Tel. 0207/405 2127; open Mon–Sat 10am–5pm; admission charged).

LONDON'S VILLAGES

Most Londoners will tell you that their city is actually a group of individual villages connected into one huge urban center. Each of these areas have their own self-contained centers, with a high (main) street, pubs, churches, grand mansions, and humbler terrace homes, cobble-stoned mews, and their own brand of local character. There are far too many of these neighborhoods to discuss here, but here are six former villages that have retained a bit of their own flavor, and that you may find interesting to explore.

Knightsbridge

Knightsbridge lies on either side of the Brompton Road, from Hyde Park on the north and toward Chelsea and South Kensington at the south and west borders. Between the park and the busy Brompton Road, you'll find a quiet, charming little enclave of mews houses and grand stucco-fronted 19th-century houses. This "village" of Knightsbridge is one of the most expensive expanses of real estate in London and is inhabited by oil-rich sheiks, aristocrats, and extremely successful business people, most of whom could tell you that "Knightsbridge" is the only word in the English language with six consonants in a row.

Harrods (see also page 83) is probably the world's most famous store. Opened by Henry Charles Harrod in 1849 as a small grocer's shop, the present terracotta palace, with its famous façade lit by some 11,000 light bulbs, was built at the turn of the century. The best attraction of the store is the Edwardian **Food Halls,** exquisitely decorated with 1,902 tiles and featuring a variety of prepared and fresh international foods, and various eateries.

West of Harrods and its vastly more fashionable neighbor, Harvey Nichols, is **Beauchamp Place** (oddly enough, pronounced "Beecham"). The former village high street is now a high fashion street with some very pricey restaurants and designer shops. **Sloane Street,** the main shopping artery, converges with the wide avenue running parallel to Hyde Park known as Knightsbridge.

Kensington

Kensington skirts the eponymous red brick palace full of royal "grace-and-favor" apartments, where the Princess of Wales lived. **Kensington Palace** has been a royal household

ever since the asthmatic William of Orange fled polluted, damp Whitehall. The State Rooms provide an interesting self-guided tour with audio tape commentary, and the Orangery nearby serves a good tea. The palace grounds became the lovely **Kensington Gardens.** Just a few yards from this peaceful world is the hustle and bustle

The world-famous Harrods Department Store began as a humble grocery in 1849.

of **Kensington High Street,** where chain stores have come to outnumber the smaller businesses, and traffic is dreadful all day long. If you take a few steps off this main thoroughfare, however, you'll find elegant squares with gorgeous old houses. Next to the neo-Gothic church of St. Mary Abbots, is **Kensington Church Street,** famous for its antiques shops. Perhaps peacocks are more to your liking than the pelicans of St. James's. Go along to **Holland Park** at the western end of Kensington High Street, to see this small jewel of a park. It's the magic garden of the blitzed Jacobean mansion that stands in the center of the park, and it contains a Japanese garden, a number of rabbits and fowl, and plenty of peacocks.

South Kensington

"South Ken" is known for its museums, a legacy of the Great Exhibition of 1851, in which Prince Albert raised money to make this the "museumland" of London. The **Victoria and Albert Museum** (called the "V&A") is the best known and biggest, but the **Natural History Museum** is worth a visit, especially for the extraordinary building in which it's housed, and the **Science Museum** is flat out fascinating. South Kensington also has a large French population, which makes for some very good patisseries. There are plenty of restaurants, hotels, and shops, as well as good transportation here, which makes it a favorite neighborhood for locals and for tourists.

The **Victoria and Albert Museum** (on Cromwell Road) houses one of the most comprehensive collections of fine and decorative arts in the world. Its 13 kilometers (8 miles) of corridors and 5 hectares (12 acres) of galleries might seem overwhelming, but for those who stick with it, it can be highly rewarding. Take a free guided tour to get you started.

The V&A houses a wide variety of sculpture, furniture, clothing, glasswork, tapestries, and painting, a crazy salad of a collection from all eras, including the present. The Cast Court is full of masterful reproductions, including a copy of Michelangelo's Statue of David, and there is a room of Raphaël cartoons that should not be missed. Be sure to stop in at the Poynter, Gamble, and Morris rooms to see what museum dining used to be like.

Next to the V&A is the **Science Museum** (Exhibition Road). If the V&A is a traditional "look, don't touch" museum, the Science Museum is very much the opposite. Many of the wonders of science are literally within your grasp as you push a button here or pull a lever there. However, with exhibits as impressive as *Puffing Billy* (the oldest surviving locomotive in the world), Stephenson's famous *Rocket*, Amy Johnson's *Gipsy Moth,* and *Apollo 10*, just looking is also a pleasure.

The fascinating **Wellcome Museum of the History of Medicine** on the top floor justifies the entrance fee to the Science Museum alone. Leave the children at "Launch Pad," where there are dozens of experiments for budding young Einsteins, while you learn about trepanning and other medical techniques which will make your hair stand on end.

The adjacent **Natural History Museum** (Cromwell Road) completes this extraordinary concentration of learning. As in the case of Science Museum, it too has become "hands-on," and its newest gallery is devoted to ecological issues. Your abiding memories, however, are likely to be of the building itself — an awesome terracotta, Romanesque "cathedral," and of its largest inhabitants: a life-size model of a blue whale measuring nearly 28 meters (93 feet) long, and dinosaur skeletons towering up to 5 meters (16 feet) above you.

Chelsea

Chelsea has been at the cutting edge of London fashion for decades. Mary Quant started it with the first boutique (long-gone) on the **King's Road,** and from the World's End (at the west end of King's Road) avant-garde designer Vivienne Westwood and Malcolm McLaren (manager of the Sex Pistols) gave the world the punk craze in the late seventies. Chelsea in the nineties is rather more subdued, and the King's Road tends nowadays towards chain stores and the odd idiosyncratic boutique, but a walk along it always provides good people-watching.

The V&A — one of the most extensive collections of fine and applied arts in the world.

Some of the brightest garments are in fact worn by the area's oldest and most conservative residents, the **Chelsea Pensioners.** Everyday attire is a navy blue uniform, but when attending events as guests of honor they dress in their famous scarlet coats, whose design dates to the 18th century. Their home is the **Royal Hospital,** a landmark in Chelsea since 1692, best approached from Royal Avenue.

Between the Hospital and the Embankment, the well-tended lawns of Ranelagh Gardens host the world-famous **Chelsea Flower Show** every spring

Continue down to the River Thames along Royal Hospital Road and turn into **Tite Street.** This attractive residential area is the very picture of bourgeois respectability, but a century ago it was a very bohemian neighborhood. Look out for the blue plaques on Tite Street dedicated to Oscar Wilde (number 34), John Singer Sargent (number 31), and Augustus John (number 33). Turn right on to the Embankment and a few yards along is **Cheyne Walk.** These splendid houses were on the water's edge until the reclamation of the Embankment in the 19th century. Blue plaques mark the former homes of pre-Raphaelite painter Dante Gabriel Rosetti as well as the author George Eliot. **Carlyle's House** (24 Cheyne Row; Tel. 0207/352 7087) is a perfect representation of a Victorian writer and thinker's house. Turned into a museum fifteen years after his death, it is almost exactly as he left it. It is open from April through October Wednesday to Sunday from 11am to 5pm; there is an admission charge.

Perhaps the most famous Chelsea resident of all was Sir Thomas More, who settled by the riverside in 1523. A plaque some hundred yards up Beaufort Street marks the site of his house. In 1535 he was taken by boat to trial at Westminster and eventually beheaded on Tower Hill for refusing to accept the "Oath of Supremacy," by which Henry VIII claimed himself equal to God. Sir Thomas intended **All Saints Church** (off Cheyne Walk) to be his

Inside and out — the Natural History Museum is guaranteed to impress.

final resting place, but his tomb actually contains his wife, Alice, as his head was taken to Canterbury.

Hampstead

Hampstead is arguably the most delightful of central London's villages and has long been home to artists and intellectuals. Lord Byron, John Keats, H.G. Wells, Robert Louis Stevenson, D.H. Lawrence, and John Constable all lived here.

The chief beauty of Hampstead is the 324-hectare (800-acre) **Hampstead Heath,** which has attracted Londoners in search of fresh air and relaxation since the 16th century, and to which Londoners fled during outbreaks of the plague. The views from the Heath and Parliament Hill are extraordinary, with London sprawling at your feet. The center of the village is full of lovely narrow lanes with immaculately tended houses and gardens. Three that are open to the public are: the **Freud Museum** (20 Maresfield Gardens, Tel. 0207/435-2002) which was the home of the father of psychoanalysis; **Keats's House,** (Wentworth Place, Keats Grove, Tel. 0207/435-2062) which is now a museum dedicated to the tragic poet; and **Fenton House,** (Windmill Hill, Tel. 0207/435-3471) a 17th-century building with fine furniture, works of art, and early musical instruments, also a museum (closed Nov–Feb). Much of Hampstead's charm lies in the small details that are easy to miss (a blue plaque here, a hidden garden of someone famous there) so the best way to see it is on a guided walking tour.

To the north of the Heath is **Kenwood House** (Hampstead Lane; Tel. 0208/348 1286), one of the most important country houses in the capital. It is an example of Palladian splendor, having been remodeled by Robert Adam in 1764. Kenwood's superb architecture and its magnificent collection of paintings (including works by Rembrandt, Turner, and Gainsborough) are worth the trip to Hampstead alone. In the summer, there are excellent outdoor concerts that can be enjoyed along with a picnic on the grass; the house is open from 10am to 6pm (only to 4pm from November to March), and admission is free.

To the east of Hampstead Heath is London's most famous final resting place, **Highgate Cemetery.** To visit the over-grown romantic western section you must join one of the hour-long tours, which depart on the hour. The most famous grave, that of Karl Marx, lies in the less interesting modern eastern section.

Southwark

Once a notorious district of brothels and Fagin-like gangs of criminals, Southwark is now a wonderful place to explore, and home to the famous recreation of **Shakespeare's Globe Theatre and Exhibition** (New Globe Walk). During the sum-mer months, you can see plays of the Bard performed in the open air, at a theater that is so faithful a reproduction of the original, actual antique tools and 450-year-old methods were used in its creation. Every detail is unassailably accurate (with the wise exception of the fire sprinkler system on the thatched roof). A fascinating museum is open year-round to tell the story of the original theater and its reconstruction.

The new **Tate Modern** (25 Sumner Street) is a recent addi-tion to the culture of the southern bank of the Thames created to house the modern art from the Tate Gallery on the north bank. There is a foot bridge being built that you can take over the Thames to the Tate Modern, which will presumably be open at the same time as the museum, on 12 May 2000.

The *Golden Hind* (St. Mary Overie Dock, Cathedral Street) is a replica of Sir Francis Drake's 16th-century ship. It has a surprising design, considering the lengths of the earth it sailed.

With manta rays, sharks, fish, and more — the London Aquarium is educational and entertaining for all ages.

Guided tours must be booked, but self-guided tours are available from 10am to 6pm. The **Clink Prison Museum** (1 Clink St.) is a rather paltry recreation of a couple of cells on the site of the original Clink Prison, a private holding tank of the corrupt Bishops of Winchester, who held sway in this district. **Southwark Cathedral,** on Montague Close near London Bridge, features a magnificent stained glass window of Shakespeare's characters. Parts of the church are from the 12th century. The **London Dungeon** (see page 70) is a theme park of gore, focusing on the bloody history of London.

LONDON FOR CHILDREN

While a capital city isn't always the best place to take a child, the diversity of children's attractions and the number of parks in London assure the little ones of an entertaining and worthwhile time. In addition to the attractions listed below, which cater specifically for children, the majority of even London's most august institutions have started to provide more fun for children, with museum trails, interactive exhibits, and children's activity carts on weekends.

The **London Zoo,** at the northern end of Regent's Park (Tel. 0207/722-3333), has long been a favorite with children. Highlights include the aviary, the reptile house, and the aquarium. The gift shops are excellent. It is open daily from 10am to 5pm; there is a substantial admission charge.

For the very young, there is nothing so riveting as the **London Aquarium** (County Hall, Westminster Bridge Road, Tel. 0207/967 8000) on the South Bank. Filled with underwater life of all descriptions, plus a wonderful petting tank filled with manta rays, it offers an agreeable time for all. And the shark tank is sure to entertain the older kids. It is open from 10am to 6pm, and there is an admission charge.

The "horrors" of Madame Tussauds seem like mere pranks in comparison with some of the goings-on at the **London Dungeon** (34 Tooley Street; Tel. 0207/403 0606). Set deep in spooky, dark, dripping vaults beneath the South Bank end of the London Bridge, the world's first horror museum is not for the very young or sensitive. Naturally, teenagers love the wax tableaux — graphic portrayals of such quaint old English customs as the rack, execution by boiling in water, burning, and hanging, not to mention drawing and quartering. Hours are 10am to 5:30pm daily, until 6:30pm during the summer; there is an admission charge.

At the **Tower of London** (see page 81) the keen sense of history evoked by the beefeaters with their picture-book costumes and colorful stories, plus the wonderful exhibits and ancient buildings, fascinate children, even those too young to understand just how important an historical site it is.

London has two fascinating museums of childhood toys and related items, although they may be even more interest-

Essentials for Attractions Outside of Central London

Kew

Royal Botanical Gardens at Kew. Kew, Surrey; Tel. 0208/940 1171. Open 9:30am–4:40pm in winter, closes 7:30pm in summer. Admission £5. The entrance from the tube station is Victoria Gate on Kew Road.

Greenwich

Cutty Sark and Gipsy Moth. King William Walk, SE10; Tel. 0208/858 3445. May–Sept Mon–Sat 10am–6pm, Sun noon–6pm; Oct–March closes 5pm. Adult £3.50, child £2.50.

Millennium Dome. north Greenwich, SE10; Tel. 0870/606 2000 (to book tickets) or 0207/808 8308 (for information). Hours and prices for the year 2000 only. Daily 10am–6pm, with evening sessions scheduled from April 2000. Adult £20, child £16.50, under 5 yrs. free.

National Maritime Museum. Romney Road, SE10; Tel. 0208/858 4422. Daily 10am–5pm. Adults £5, child £2.50, under 5 yrs free.

Royal Greenwich Observatory. Greenwich Park, SE10; Tel. 0208/858 4422. Daily 10am–5pm. Adult £2.50, child £1.

Royal Naval College. King William Walk (off Romney Rod. SE10, Tel. 0208/858 2154. Daily 2:30pm–4:45pm. Free.

Thames Flood Barrier Visitors Centre. Unity Way, Woolwich, SE18; Tel. 0208/305 4188. Mon–Fri 10am–5pm, Sat–Sun 10:30am–5:30pm. Adult £3.40, child £2.40.

Hampton Court

Hampton Court Palace. Mid-March–mid-Oct Mon 10:15am–6pm, Tue–Sun 9:30am–6pm; mid-Oct–mid-March closes 4:30pm. Adult £10, child £6.60, under 5 yrs. free.

Windsor

Windsor Castle. Castle Hill, Windsor; Tel. 01753/868 286. March–Oct daily 10am–5:30pm, Nov–Feb daily 10am–4pm. Call before visiting as sudden closures are frequent. Adult £10, child £5, under 5 yrs. free.

ing to the adults in the group. The biggest is the **Bethnal Green Museum of Childhood** (Cambridge Heath Rd., E2; Tel. 0208//980 4315), created from the V&A's fabled overflow of treasures. It claims to be the largest public collection of dolls' houses, games, and puppets on view anywhere in the world (open 10am–5:50pm, closed Friday, free admission). It is located slightly out of the center of London in the East End, across from the Bethnal Green underground station.

By contrast **Pollock's Toy Museum** (1 Scala St., W1; Tel. 0207/636 3452) is a mere toy box housed in two small adjoining houses dating from 1760. Visiting it is a bit like stumbling upon childhood memories in granny's attic, and is one of London's most charming places. The museum is open daily from 10am to 5pm. There is an admission charge.

For great toys to take home as gifts, try **Hamleys** in Regent Street (see page 54). This is a huge toy store and it's always very busy, so don't expect a quick visit. Covent Garden is excellent for small, high-quality craft and toy shops, and the buskers here will keep the whole family amused.

For teens there's the state-of-the-art attraction by the Madame Tussauds organization: the **Rock Circus** (see page 80). Short-wave headphones pick up the music as you walk past static wax figures of rock heroes and the rousing finale is a show which features audio-animatronic models of some of the world's greatest rock musicians, past and present.

And last but not least there's the fun-for-the-whole-family **British Airways London Eye** (see page 79).

DAY TRIPS

London's best-loved day trips all lie within 34 km (21 miles) of the center of town. The Royal Botanic Gardens at Kew is 11 km (7 miles) away, but still on the underground line (Kew Gardens). Greenwich is 8 km (5 miles) from central London,

Explore the grand maritime history of Greenwich and its surrounding sights, such as the Millennium Dome.

reachable by the Docklands Light Railway, train from Charing Cross, or even boat down the Thames. Hampton Court Palace is 23 km (14 miles) by British Rail from Waterloo or by Green Line bus. Windsor is 40 km (25 miles) by British Rail from Paddington or Waterloo or by Green Line bus. Package tours may cram two, or even all, of these into one day, but try to resist the temptation. Each can make a day out in its own right, with riverside pubs, tearooms, restaurants, and quaint shops, as well as leafy surroundings, to enjoy at your leisure.

The Royal Botanic Gardens, Kew

These famous gardens were founded in 1759 by Princess Augusta (mother of George III) and laid out by that legendary gardener Lancelot "Capability" Brown.

A combination of research center and public pleasure gardens, they cover over 116 hectares (288 acres) and contain over 25,000 species and varieties of plant. There are three primary glasshouses to visit — the **Princess of Wales Conservatory,** representing modern Kew, the **Palm House,** and the **Temperate House,** the latter two being magnificent Victorian crystal palaces. **Kew Palace,** near the main gate, is the smallest of all the royal palaces in England. The **Orangerie,** built in 1761, now houses a gift shop and restaurant.

Greenwich

Greenwich, long the favored destination of nautical and science buffs, is prepared for an onslaught of tourists heading straight for the **Millennium Dome.** Opened to the public on 1 January 2000, the much-maligned, much-hyped celebration of the millennium that is meant to rival the Great Exhibition of 1851. Twice the size of Wembley Stadium, the Dome has 14 themed zones that will examine the human body and brain, aiming specifically at the identity of 21st-century Britons: how they work, play, communicate, travel, create, and take care of their resources. The exhibit will be open for only a year.

All that modernism crowding the tip of Greenwich makes the traditional sights of the area that much more quaint in comparison. Take a boat there from Westminster or the Tower to reach Greenwich in the time-honored way: along the river Thames. Hard by the pier rise the tall and graceful masts of the *Cutty Sark;* climb aboard to explore the last of the British sailing clippers, now in dry dock. Adjacent to the *Cutty Sark* is the diminutive *Gipsy Moth IV,* in which Sir Francis Chichester became the first Englishman to sail around the world single-handed in 1966. Both are located on St. William Walk, near the Greenwich Pier.

It's an uphill climb from the pier to the **Royal Observatory, Greenwich** (formerly known as the "Old Royal Observatory"). The complex takes in Flamsteed House, a Wren building of 1675 that housed several Astronomer Royals and their equipment. As England's most important naval observation site, Greenwich became the world's zero meridian of longitude in 1884. The observatory ceased to function in the 1930s when smog and city lights forced it out into the Sussex countryside, and the building now houses a museum.

The **National Maritime Museum** is the world's largest museum of its kind. There is too much to take in all in one visit, but don't miss the Neptune Hall and the Barge House, where full-size craft include an 18th-century royal barge. The **Royal Naval College** occupies the Baroque buildings of the former Royal Naval Hospital. You can visit the Grand Hall and the Chapel (afternoons only, closed Thursday).

There is plenty more to see in Greenwich: the Fan Museum, the 17th-century Ranger's House, and the excellent weekend market (College Approach; during the Summer there is an outdoor market on Greenwich High Street). Join

*Windsor Castle has long been a symbol of English pride —
Here's a detailed look at the Tudor-style residences.*

a guided tour, setting off from the Tourist Information Centre between noon and 2pm Tuesday through Sunday.

Boats leave regularly from Greenwich for the 25-minute trip to the **Thames Barrier.** As you head downriver, the salty tang of the sea may hit you and you realize that the Thames, with its industrial landscape of smokestacks and cranes, is still a working river. It can also be a lethal force, as it last proved in 1953 when 14 people were drowned in their basements as far upstream as Westminster. To ensure London would never be flooded again, the £450-million Thames Barrier was built between 1975 and 1982. An audio-visual presentation explains how it works and tours show you the Barrier close up.

☛ Windsor Castle

Windsor Castle is the same vintage as the Tower of London, and is one of a circle of forts built by William the Conqueror,

The gallant Queen's Guards on their way to the Changing of the Guard — England's most time-honored ceremony.

one day's march from London. The royal standard flies when the Sovereign is in residence, and there is a Changing of the Guard ceremony at 11am.

Picturesque in the extreme, the world's largest occupied castle sprawls on top of a bluff with a commanding view over the Thames. The walled precinct is divided into lower, middle, and upper wards, which are dominated by the chesspiece Round Tower, built in 1170. Additions were made piecemeal through the centuries, in particular St. George's Chapel (1478–1511) and the luxurious State Apartments. The restoration project from the devastating fire of 1992 was an amazing feat of craftsmanship, and the exhibition about the six-year effort is as fascinating as the results are stunning.

St. George's Chapel is the architectural *tour de force* of the castle. This fine example of the Perpendicular style ranks on a par with the Henry VII Chapel in Westminster Abbey.

The other glory of the castle is the suite of **State Apartments,** decorated with carved and gilded furniture from France and England, Gobelins tapestries, masterpieces by Rubens and van Dyck, and ceiling scenes by Antonio Verrio. The State Apartments are closed when the Queen is in Official Residence, from March to early May, most of June, and over Christmas and the New Year. There may be some special occasions that call for the castle to be closed to the public, so be sure to check before heading out.

Finally, don't miss the incredible **Queen Mary's Dolls' House.** It was designed by Sir Edwin Lutyens, and its contents include real Wedgwood china, a tiny working Hoover, and functioning lighting and plumbing.

The streets below the castle have more than their fair share of cheap touristy shops and mediocre restaurants, and in summer become very crowded. Escape across the bridge to **Eton,** where the famous elite public (i.e., *private*) school has been in existence for more than 550 years, producing no less than 20 British Prime Ministers. Prince William and Prince Harry both go to Eton, where their royal status doesn't so much as raise an eyebrow among the other sons of aristocratic families. Inquire at the tourist information office (near Windsor and Eton Central railway station) about tours of the school.

☛ Hampton Court Palace

This beautiful red-brick Tudor mansion lies 23 km (14 miles) west of central London. It is undoubtedly the most romantic of London's royal palaces, and the majority of it is open to the general public.

Built in 1514 for Cardinal Wolsey, it was appropriated by Henry VIII in 1525, following Wolsey's fall from grace. It was Henry's favorite palace, and he spent five of his six honeymoons here. You enter through the Great Gatehouse (built during the 1530s), which leads on to Base Court and Anne Boleyn's Gateway. Inside is a magnificent astronomical clock made for King Henry VIII in 1540. It shows the hour, day, month, phases of the Moon, and even the state of the tides, and is wrought with meticulous beauty.

The **State Apartments** are some of the most sumptuous of any royal palace, featuring works by such great and gifted craftsmen as Grinling Gibbons, Antonio Verrio, and William Kent. Wolsey's Closet is a remarkably well-preserved study lined with delicate linenfold wooden paneling. The highlights, however, are the **Great Hall** and the **Chapel Royal.**

If you would like to keep the children amused for an hour or two, take them to the famous **Maze,** which has been baffling royalty and visitors for some 300 years. The paths within the maze wind around and around for almost a kilometer (about half a mile).

Essentials for Attractions in Central London

Banqueting House. Whitehall, SW1; Tel. 0207/ 930 4179. Mon–Sat 10am–5pm. Adult £3.50, child £2.50. Call before visiting as sudden closures are frequent.

British Airways London Eye (The Ferris Wheel). On Thames outside County Hall, SE1; Tel. 0207/707 4159. Daily Apr–Oct 9am–10pm, Nov–Mar 10am–6pm. Adult £7.45, child £4.95.

British Museum. Great Russell St., W1; Tel. 0207/636-1555. Mon–Sat 10am–6pm, Sun. 2:30pm–6pm. Free.

Buckingham Palace. SW1; Tel. 0207/839 1377. Aug–Sept daily 9:30am–4:30pm. Adult £10, child £5, under 5 yrs. free.

Clink Prison Museum. 1 Clink St. SE1; Tel. 0207/378 1558; Daily 10am–6pm. Adult £4, concessions £3.

Courtauld Institute Galleries. Somerset House, Strand, WC2; Tel. 0207/873 2526. Mon–Sat 10am–6pm. Adult £4, child free.

Fenton House. Windmill Hill, Hampstead, NW3; Tel. 0207/435 3471. Apr–Oct Wed–Fri 2–5pm, Sat–Sun 11am–5pm. Adults £4.

Freud Museum. 20 Maresfield Gardens, Hampstead, NW3; Tel. 0207/435 2002. Wed–Sun noon–5pm. Adults £3, child free.

Golden Hind. St Mary Overie Dock, Cathedral St., SE1; Tel. 0870/011 8700. Daily 10am–6pm. Adult £2.30 for self-guided tour, £2.80 for guided tour (must be arranged in advance).

Highgate Cemetery. Swan's Lane, Hampstead, N6; Tel. 0208/340 1834. *West Cemetery:* Guided tours Mon–Fri noon, 2pm & 4pm, Sat–Sun hourly 11am–4pm. Admission £3; *East Cemetery:* Apr–Sept 10am–5 pm, Oct–Mar 10am–4pm. Admission £1.

The Palace of Westminster (Houses of Parliament). Parliament Sq., SW1; Tel. 0207/219 3000. Free. Call well in advance to find out when it will be possible to attend a session. Parliament is generally in session Nov–Mar with recesses at Christmas and Easter.

Dr. Johnson's House. 17 Gough St., EC4; Tel. 0207/353 3745. Mon–Sat 11am–5pm. Adult £3, Child £1.

Keats's House. Keats Grove, Hampstead, NW3. Apr–Oct Mon–Fri 10am–1pm & 2–6pm, Sat until 5pm, Sun 2–5pm; Nov–Mar Mon–Fri 1–5pm, Sat 10am–1pm & 2–5pm, Sun 2–5pm. Free.

Kensington Palace. Kensington Gardens, W8; Tel. 0207/937 9561. May–Sept daily 10am–6pm, Oct–April daily 10am–4pm. Adult £9.50, child £7.10.

London Transport Museum. The Piazza, Covent Garden, WC 2; Tel. 0171/565 7299. Daily 10am–6pm. (Friday from 11am). Adult £5.50, child £2.95

Madame Tussauds Wax Museum. Marylebone Rd., NW1; Tel. 0207/935 6861. Daily 10am–5:30pm. Adult £9.50, child £6.25, under 4 yrs. free.

Madame Tussauds Rock Circus. London Pavilion, Piccadilly Circus, W1; Tel. 0207/734 7203. Daily 10am–5:30pm (Tues from 11am). Adult £8.25, child £6.25.

National Gallery. Trafalgar Square, WC2; Tel. 020/7839 3321 (020/7839 3526 for recorded information). Mon–Sat 10am–6pm (Wed until 8pm), Sun noon–5:50pm. Free.

National Portrait Gallery. 2 St. Martin's Place, WC2; Tel. 0207/306 0055. Mon–Sat 10am–6pm, Sun noon–6pm. Free.

Natural History Museum. Cromwell Rd., SW7; Tel. 0207/938 9123. Mon–Sat 10am–5:50pm. Adult £6.50, child free.

Royal Academy of Art. Burlington House, Piccadilly, W1; Tel. 0207/439 7438. Daily 10am–6pm. Adult £5.50, child £2.50.